Praise for

Morning Devotionals: "Inspired to Press Forward"
31 Devotions & Declarations That Will Inspire You to Press Forward, By Faith

Minister Bernard Marrow is an admirable, faithful steward of God, whose unique style and daily devotions will connect readers with the heart of God. Readers will be blessed by the intimate words written in this book. During these times, the people of God need daily guidance in discipleship, stewardship, and worship. Minister Bernard Marrow, through the inspiration of the Holy Spirit, has provided a literary gem for today's world to "press forward."

Deacon Jermaine Worthy
New Salem Baptist Church
Philadelphia, PA

"Inspired to Press Forward" is a powerful and inspiring work that truly exemplifies **Proverbs 18:21 "Life and death is in the power of the tongue and they that love it shall eat the fruit thereof."** Each of the thirty-one morning prayers and declarations is based on the Scriptures and is designed to encourage the reader to speak life concerning their success, deliverance, and victory.

The main theme of this book is to "press forward." That term implies forward progress, regardless of life's circumstances, obstacles, or *struggles. We serve a progressive God who is always moving forward, making a way, and working things out for us. That same God has not called us to be stagnant or to retreat, but to press forward boldly in Jesus' Name. In the words of Minister Marrow, we are challenged to "**get** in position," "**stay** in position," and "**own** the position!"*

*The second part of the book motivates the reader to take action by giving insight on how to press forward by faith, how to press forward through challenges, and how to press forward to be exactly who God has created you to be and to be successful at it! In times such as these, we cannot afford to be hearers only of the Word of God — we must be doers as well. I believe "Inspired to Press Forward" sets the tone and helps to propel the reader into action. "Inspired to Press Forward" encourages us to "keep **pressing**," "keep **praising**," and keep **praying**!" After reading this book, I am even more inspired to continue to press forward by faith, and I believe this book will motivate you to do the same.*

Evangelist Cheryl A. Johnson
Founder and President
The Women in the Word Ministries
Philadelphia, PA

Morning Devotionals

INSPIRED TO PRESS FORWARD

*31 DEVOTIONS & DECLARATIONS
THAT WILL INSPIRE YOU
TO PRESS FORWARD,
BY FAITH*

Minister Bernard Marrow

BFWG Ministry

In Conjunction with

Morning Devotionals: *"Inspired to Press Forward"*
31 Devotions & Declarations That Will Inspire You to Press Forward, By Faith by Minister Bernard Marrow

Cover design, editing, book layout, and publishing services by KishKnows, Inc., Richton Park, Illinois, 708-252-DOIT admin@kishknow.com, www.kishknows.com

ISBN:978-0-578-77659-0
LCCN:2020921157

All rights reserved. No part of this book may be reproduced, distributed, or transmitted in any form or by any means, including photocopying, recording, digital scanning, or other electronic or mechanical methods, without the prior written permission of the publisher, except in the case of brief quotations embodied in critical reviews and certain other noncommercial uses permitted by copyright law. For permission requests, please contact Minister Bernard Marrow at connectwithmin.marrow@gmail.com.

Some Scripture references may be paraphrased versions or illustrative references of the author. Unless otherwise specified, all other references are from King James Version of the Bible.

Some Scripture quotations are taken from **THE MESSAGE**, Copyright© 1993, 2002, 2018 by Eugene H. Peterson. Used by permission of NavPress. All rights reserved. Represented by Tyndale House Publishers, Inc.

THE HOLY BIBLE, NEW INTERNATIONAL VERSION®, **NIV®** Copyright© 1973, 1978, 1984, 2011 by Biblica, Inc.® Used by permission. All rights reserved worldwide.

Copyright © 2020 by Bernard Marrow
Printed in the United States of America

Table of Contents

Praise for
Morning Devotionals:
"Inspired to Press Forward"
31 Devotions & Declarations That Will Inspire You to Press Forward, By Faith

Acknowledgments	ix
About This Book	xi
Introduction	xiii
31 Morning Devotionals **"Inspired to Press Forward"**	1-65
How to Press Forward By Faith	67
How to Press Forward Through All Challenges	69
How to Press Forward to Be Exactly Who God Created You to Be	73
How to Press Forward to Win!	77
My Testimony	81
Conclusion	83
Testimonials	85
About the Ministry	87
About the Author	89
Connect with the Author	93

Acknowledgments

First, giving honor to God who is truly first in my life. I'm grateful for all that He has done in my life...where He's brought me from, for where He has me, for where He's leading me, and for the purpose that He has assigned to my life to fulfill.

Throughout this process, I also truly thank God for those who stuck by my side:

My wife, Vanessa Marrow, who showed me love, inspired me, and encouraged me to stay focused.

My mom, Joyce Marrow, and sister, Belinda Marrow, who showed me an abundance of love and support.

All those who have helped me and were obedient to God, supporting and encouraging me along the way. I love you all so much!

THANK YOU, JESUS! I LOVE HIM THE MOST!

In Loving Memory of

Rev. Robert T. Moore Jr.
August 5, 1957 – March 30, 2020

Pastor of the New Salem Baptist Church in Philadelphia, PA and my spiritual father, who always showed me an abundance of love and support and helped groom me into the man that I am today. Forever and always in my heart. I love you, Pop!

About This Book

Morning Devotionals:
"Inspired to Press Forward"
31 Devotions & Declarations That Will Inspire You to Press Forward, By Faith is a devotional that you can pick up each morning as you spend time in the Word of God. It is designed to inspire you to press forward with the Word of God as your foundation, helping you to stay focused and grounded on who God is, and what He says in His Word.

Introduction

For the past five years, I have been blessed to be able to share encouragement and inspiration with the children of God each morning, blessing them through His Word, as well as what He gives me through the Holy Spirit.

Every week, Monday through Friday, God has used me to send out a morning message to over one hundred people via text message and to post on all of the major social media channels. My prayer is that every message and prayer will encourage you all to press forward, knowing that God is always with you, that He'll always have you covered, and that you can give Him all the glory!

Every day of our lives, we wake up facing challenges, difficulties, obstacles, and family and relational issues. At times, they may be difficult to deal with, and you may feel as though you're all alone, left to figure things out by yourself. The people around you, who are supposed to be there to help, inspire, encourage, and keep you focused, may not be as supportive as you thought they would. Thank God for those who do step up…still, at times, it may seem that there's no way out when your situation remains the same.

With these Scriptures and inspirational readings, you can learn about who God is and the love He has for you. The promises He's made to you are guaranteed to be fulfilled in your life when you *"Walk by faith, and not by sight."* **(2 Corinthians 5:7 KJV)**

I encourage you to *"Look to the hills from whence cometh your help"* because *"Your help cometh from the Lord who made heaven and earth."* **(Psalm 121:1-2 KJV)** I am telling you what a friend we have in Jesus, who cares for you and loves you unconditionally. His love is unfailing and never-ending. I want you to know that because God is the greatest power, we shall never be defeated! As you read this devotional, know that when you have a strong faith, you'll always have a strong finish! Why? Because believing the message of Jesus Christ is the only way to develop a strong faith. We must hear it, receive it, believe it, and confess it—by faith! The Word of God equips us for this life. It is the breath of God, and it is everything that we need to live. Jesus said, *"The words I speak to you are life."* **(John 6:63 KJV)** Above all else, we need the Word of God planted in our hearts because otherwise, we will not grow in faith, which *"comes by hearing and hearing by the Word of God."* The more you read the Word of God, the more you become familiar with Jesus Christ and grow in faith!

DAY ONE

*"Then spake Jesus again unto them, saying,
I am the light of the world:
he that followeth me shall not walk in darkness,
but shall have the light of life."*
John 8:12 (KJV)

Morning Prayer/Declaration:

Decree and declare over yourself: *"I command my day to be great! No weapon formed against me shall prosper, and I will rise above every difficulty, knowing that God has given me the power to overcome. I will see **Ephesians 3:20** exceedingly and abundantly above and beyond all that I ask or think of. I will trust that what I cannot make happen on my own, God will make happen for me. I've got victory in Jesus, and there's nothing the enemy can do about it!"* Speak it. Believe it. Receive it.

Jesus is the light of the world. The Anointed One who shines through us and illuminates our paths. Light always drives out the darkness; and when we open our lives to the light of Jesus, the enemy has to flee, and we are free to shine brightly. God will use your freedom and light to bring freedom to others, for His Glory.

Many times in the Bible, Jesus says, *"I Am"* and then gives a description. He describes Himself as the *door **(John 10:7)***, the *bread of life **(John 6:35)***, the *way, the truth, and the life **(John 14:6)***, and the *resurrection and the life **(John 11:25)***. Over and over, He defines Himself. You discover *who* you are by knowing *whose* you are. Jesus knew *who* He was and *why* He was here.

As you pray and press your way today, realize the true identity of Christ. Profess your identity in Christ, and affirm the mission and purpose that He has assigned to you to fulfill. Comprehend your ability as followers of Christ, and utilize the gifts that you have been given. Follow Christ, and let Him be the light in your life.

#ByFaithWeGood

DAY TWO

"And be not conformed to this world: but be ye transformed by the renewing of your mind, that ye may prove what is that good, and acceptable, and perfect, will of God."
Romans 12:2 (KJV)

Morning Prayer/Declaration:

Decree and declare over yourself: *God's plan for my life is coming to pass, and it will not be stopped by people, disappointments, or adversities. God has solutions to every problem I will ever face already lined up, and the right people and the right breaks are in my future. I will fulfill my destiny. Speak it. Believe it. Receive it.*

How do you do this? The Bible says that God transforms you into a new person by changing the way you think. When you let go of small thinking and stop limiting God, you will open up your life to your dreams and the fullness of His blessings. Once that happens, you find yourself no longer conforming to the pattern of the world but to the will of God. Our *behavior* will change when our *thinking* changes.

We are chosen and set apart because we are different…and we need to take ownership of *how* different we really are. Being citizens of Heaven, we don't have to get caught up in religion. Believe in *relationship* over *religion,* and choose *faith* over *tradition.* Have a Kingdom mindset. When we have a personal relationship with Jesus Christ, we begin to know Him intimately, and there is a change that begins to take place in our lives. We begin to make decisions that are based on who we are in Christ Jesus. Be encouraged and press forward, knowing that through Him, all things are possible.

#ByFaithWeGood

DAY THREE

"Now faith is the substance of things hoped for, the evidence of things not seen." ***Hebrews 11:1 (KJV)***

Morning Prayer/Declaration:

Father, today I press toward You. I believe that You have my miracle in the palm of Your hand, and I choose to take my eyes off of my circumstances and set my gaze on You because You are the Author and Finisher of my faith. In your precious name, Jesus. Amen!

Faith is…

- Being sure of what you hope for and certain of what you do not see. Being fully assured.

- The formula for the manifestation of God's Word.

- Not wavering or doubting.

- Gaining an understanding of God's Word and knowing how to apply it to your life, in every situation that comes your way.

- Speaking the Word of God and knowing that what you speak and believe, you shall receive!

- Faith *sees* the invisible, *believes* the unbelievable, and *receives* the impossible.

#ByFaithWeGood

DAY **FOUR**

*"But without faith it is impossible to please him:
for he that cometh to God must believe that he is,
and that he is a rewarder of them that diligently seek him."*
Hebrews 11:6 (KJV)

Morning Prayer/Declaration:

Father, thank you for sending your Son, Jesus, to be with us. Thank you that you didn't stay distant, but you left the beauty of heaven to come to earth to rescue us and ultimately bring us close to yourself again. Holy Spirit, teach us fully what it means that you're with us. Father, thank you for your promise to bless me with your true and lasting peace, no matter what I'm facing. In Jesus' mighty Name! Amen.

God is *always* on time. When it's your season for what God has promised and destined to you, it *will* come, and it *will* flourish. Have strong faith and trust God at all times, knowing that He is real and alive! You can't have anything without faith. It is the only thing that will get us all the way through.

Without faith, you can't even get God's attention. As you press forward, have faith that God will show up and show out on your behalf. Have faith to be healed. To be delivered. For provision. For doors to open. To overcome. Know that we have victory in Jesus!

When you pray by faith, God *listens*. When you listen, God *speaks*. When you believe, God *works. He is faithful!*

#ByFaithWeGood

DAY FIVE

*"For God hath not given us the spirit of fear;
but of power, and of love, and of a sound mind."*
2 Timothy 1:7 (KJV)

Morning Prayer/Declaration:

Decree and declare over yourself: *Everything that I set my mind to do, I will see it through. Everything that I put my hands to shall prosper. Everything that tries to hinder my steps shall be blocked. Every tongue that rises against me shall be silenced. Every thought and action shall be in alignment with God's plan for my life and come what may, every situation will work out for my good. Speak it. Believe it. Receive it.*

We have all experienced fear. Maybe you are afraid of losing your job or your finances, or maybe losing a loved one. Maybe you have a fear of loneliness or of not being accepted by others. Perhaps you fear failure or rejection. We fear for our children. Our relationships. Our inability to face the day. Whatever your fear may be, you have uttered the words, *"I am afraid"* at one time or another. Fear has a powerful influence on how we think and act…but God wants you to *live!* God has given us life through His Son, and He wants us to live free from the torment of fear.

It's a new day, which means a new *beginning*. A new *mindset*. A new *focus*. A new *start*. And new *intentions*. The Lord told me to tell you this morning: *"Don't give up. You're almost there. Keep pressing, keep praising, and keep praying! Let your faith be bigger and stronger than your fear!"*

#ByFaithWeGood

DAY SIX

*"O Lord, thou hast searched me, and known me.
Thou knowest my downsitting and mine uprising,
thou understandest my thought afar off."*
Psalm 139:1-2 (KJV)

Morning Prayer/Declaration:

It's another beautiful blessed day that God has allowed us to see! On this beautiful blessed morning, give God a "Thank You!" Decree and declare over yourself: *Today will be a great day. I will speak love, peace, and happiness.* "This is the day that the Lord has made, I will rejoice and be glad in it." **(Psalm 118:24)** *Speak* it. *Believe* it. *Receive* it.

David wrote this to declare that God knew *everything* about him...even the most everyday things such as sitting down and getting up. God not only knew the smallest aspects of David's everyday life...He also knew his *thoughts*. It is the same for us. There is nothing that we can bring to God that He doesn't already know. God is all-knowing and familiar with all of our ways.

What an awesome display of the love of God. He desires to connect with us on such a level that there is nothing He does not know about us. Don't let your fears keep you from being great for God! There is nothing happening in your life that God is not aware of, and He wants you to know that you are fully known and fully loved by Him.

If you are feeling lost, alone, and without purpose, know that God knows you and is with you always. He has not abandoned you…and He never will. God's way is the best way and you are always safe in His hands!

#ByFaithWeGood

DAY SEVEN

*"If I ascend up into heaven, thou art there:
if I make my bed in hell, behold, thou art there.
If I take the wings of the morning,
and dwell in the uttermost parts of the sea; Even there shall thy
hand lead me, and thy right hand shall hold me."*
Psalm 139:8-10 (KJV)

Morning Prayer/Declaration:

Decree and declare over yourself: *Today will be a blessed day because God is working all things together for my good. I will choose faith over fear, and I will not use my energy to worry – but to believe because what God has planned for me will succeed, and His goodness and mercy shall follow me all the days of my life. Speak it. Believe it. Receive it.*

No matter where you are in life or where you choose to go, God is there. His promises through His Word are what keeps us from losing our minds when trouble knocks at our door. They are what "keeps us keeping on" when the going gets tough. They are what causes us to shout even when the bills are not paid. What makes us sing with joy at the funeral of a loved one. They help us endure hardship, withstand betrayal, and press through setback after setback...even as we wait for our comeback.

No matter where you are, God is available *to* and *for* you, ready to lead, guide, direct, and protect you. He is holding you up with the strength that He freely provides. There is nothing you can hide from God and nowhere you can go where He is not there. Focus on who God is…His plan, His purpose, and His desire. Seek what He wants more than what you want because His way is the best way. He's always with you, and He has you covered. God is Faithful!

#ByFaithWeGood

DAY EIGHT

"For thou hast possessed my reins: thou hast covered me in my mother's womb. I will praise thee; for I am fearfully and wonderfully made: marvelous are thy works; and that my soul knoweth right well."
Psalm 139:13-14 (KJV)

Morning Prayer/Declaration:

Declare today by faith that you will succeed, and never fail! You will win, and never lose! Declare that God will *protect*, *provide for*, and *prosper* you and your family. Every situation is working for your good, and there is *nothing* that the enemy can do about it. *Speak* it. *Believe* it. *Receive* it.

God made you exactly who He wants you to be, and He loves you too much to allow you to stay tied to anyone or anything that does not bring out the best in you. As you press forward, walk in confidence and declare over yourself, *"I am who God said I am. I can be who God said I can be, and I can do what God created me to do. I can have what God says I can have because there is no limit with God, and there is nothing that the enemy can do about it. In Jesus' Name!"*

Everything that you need to be the successful person that God wants you to be is within you. You are equipped, blessed, talented, and empowered, and because of that, you can be focused, bold, and confident. Don't hold back...give God praise for who He is and for all the great things He's done! Remember...you are *fearfully* and *wonderfully* made!

#ByFaithWeGood

DAY NINE

"You watched me as I was being formed in utter seclusion, as I was woven together in the dark of the womb. You saw me before I was born. Every day of my life was recorded in your book. Every moment was laid out before a single day had passed."
Psalm 139:15-16 (NLT)

Morning Prayer/Declaration:

Declare today: *I'm still alive, and there is still time for me to see a miracle. I've got faith that God is going to do it, and there's nothing the enemy can do about it! Speak it. Believe it. Receive it.*

The days of your life are already written. God knew you before the foundation of the earth, and your victory is already set up! Your destiny is waiting for you. God has already prepared the way for you and made all of the *"crooked places straight."* **(Isaiah 45:2)** God is the *"author and finisher of your faith."* **(Hebrews 12:2)** The writer of your story. Everything you'll ever need and all that you have to accomplish. He's everywhere you need to be, and He is already set up. God has already worked everything out for your good, and every battle is already won!

Even when it is not clear which choice you should make, you can take comfort in the fact that *"It is God who is at work in you, both to will and to work for His good pleasure."* **(Philippians 2:13)** The Lord takes responsibility for directing you through tough times, and He will move heaven and earth to show you His will in His timing!

#ByFaithWeGood

DAY TEN

*"How precious are your thoughts about me, O God.
They cannot be numbered! I can't even count them;
they outnumber the grains of sand!
And when I wake up, you are still with me!"*
Psalm 139:17-18 (NLT)

*"For I know the plans I have for you," declares the Lord,
"plans to prosper you and not to harm you,
plans to give you hope and a future."*
Jeremiah 29:11 (NIV)

Morning Prayer/Declaration:

Declare today: *I speak blessings and not curses...life and not death. I speak good and not evil. Today and every day, I'm confident knowing I'm a child of the Most High God, who is protected, provided for, and strengthened; having peace, and being equipped to succeed in every situation! In Jesus' Name! Speak it. Believe it. Receive it.*

God has a plan for our lives that will benefit us and bring hope to our lives...yet some of us are so set on charting our own course that we refuse to put our lives in God's hands, and see what He has for us.

God is telling you, *"As the sand of the sea, so are my thoughts are towards you."* **(Psalm 139:18)** That's how much He loves you. In the midst of the pain, His thoughts are toward *you*. In the midst of joy, God's thoughts are toward *you*. God has thoughts toward you…because He has been weaving you together since before time began.

God wants you to be happy, and He is preparing the best for you *right now*. You can rest well knowing that the moment you decided to walk by faith and not by sight, you decided to let God take control; and *that* is when you make yourself available to receive God's best.

#ByFaithWeGood

DAY ELEVEN

*"Search me, O God, and know my heart: try me,
and know my thoughts: And see if there be
any wicked way in me, and lead me in the way everlasting."*
Psalm 139:23-24 (KJV)

Morning Prayer/Declaration:

Declare today and every day: *I will fill my heart with what is good, so that nothing bad proceeds from it. "Create in me a clean heart, oh God. And renew a right spirit within me."* **(Psalm 51:10 KJV)** *"Let the words of my mouth, and the meditation of my heart, be acceptable in thy sight, O Lord, my strength, and my redeemer."* **(Psalm 19:14 KJV)** *Speak it. Believe it. Receive it*

When we surrender our plans to Him, He takes what He knows about us and creates a purposed approach. Every day is a gift, and it's our responsibility to do something with the present moment that will honor God and the gifts and assignments He's given us. Not only has He placed in you unique gifts and talents, He's also calling you to develop the ability to recognize them. Jesus said that His plan for us is a *"life more abundant." (John 10:10)* The Amplified version calls it, *"life to the full, till it overflows."* A life well-lived, a job well-done, and a life of more abundance is one that spills over into the lives that surround you, revealing purpose to your family, colleagues, and friends and allowing them to experience the benefits of abundance in their lives as well.

God knows how many hairs are on our head, and he has each one numbered. He knit us together in our mother's womb, and He is everywhere. Don't hide from your problems—invite God into them. He knows the words before they even come out of our mouths, and in His Word, He wrote about EVERY SINGLE DAY He planned out for us before one of them had happened.

#ByFaithWeGood

DAY TWELVE

"Trust in the Lord with all thine heart; and lean not unto thine own understanding. In all thy ways acknowledge him, and he shall direct thy paths."
Proverbs 3:5-6 (KJV)

Morning Prayer/Declaration:

"Father, we thank you for another beautiful, blessed day that you have allowed us to see. Thank you for your unconditional, unfailing love. Thank you for the gift of life and the unique path that you've designed for each and every one of us. Thank you for your mercy that gently prods us in the right direction when we err. Teach us to keep our focus on the vision ahead of us, as we run in our lane and stay the course, regardless of the challenges. Grant us patience and tenacity to overcome the hurdles in our way, so that we can finish strong and earn the reward that comes with it. Be glorified in all we do. In your precious Son Jesus' Name. Amen!"

When we depend upon our own ability we fall very short. In order to be effective, we must understand that our abilities, strength, and understanding come straight from God and not from our own perspective. *"Trust in the Lord with all thine heart and lean not to thine own understanding."* God is saying that there are going to be times when it seems like the more you pray, the more you *have* to pray. Times when it seems as if you can see your vision and dreams drifting away. Sometimes, it seems as if your dreams are on hold, and your time has gone. And there will be times when the enemy will get busy, trying to destroy your character or your reputation to slow you down. Remember what God said in His Word: *"Trust in the Lord with all thine heart."* God made a promise that He will never fail us nor forsake us.

Don't focus on what you see (how your situation looks), don't listen to everything you hear, and don't do what you think you need to do. Because of God's promises, even if you can't see *how* it is going to come to pass, or you can't see *when* it is going to come to pass, know that His promises *will* come to pass!

#ByFaithWeGood

DAY THIRTEEN

"Thou wilt keep him in perfect peace, whose mind is stayed on thee: because he trusteth in thee. Trust ye in the Lord forever: for in the Lord Jehovah is everlasting strength:"
Isaiah 26:3-4 (KJV)

Morning Prayer/Declaration:

Declare: *No longer will anything take place in my life unless I allow it. I have the power and authority that God gave me, and nothing that is the opposite of who God is and against His plan will happen in my midst. I am victorious, and every situation will work for my good and for God's glory! Speak it. Believe it. Receive it.*

God's *peace* is found in God's *presence*. When we fix our eyes on Jesus, He offers us a peace that goes far beyond anything we can understand. And this peace is a daily invitation. Every single day, God offers us an opportunity to find His peace through prayer, reading His Word, listening to Him, and following His instructions. Spend some time being still in God's presence today. Think about who He is, and focus your thoughts on Him. The peace of God is an inward sense of completeness; and by keeping your mind stayed on Him and resting in His presence, you will always feel complete and at peace, knowing God is in control. Distractions will work to take away that sense of wholeness, but by trusting God completely, our peace is no longer controlled by circumstances, other people, our emotions, or our limitations. Instead, we've got God's "perfect peace."

Wherever you have to go, whatever you have to do, and whatever you may be dealing with, you will be able to keep your peace if you can keep your focus on Jesus. Focus on the truth of God and trust in the Lord, knowing that He will always lead you in the right direction and fight every battle for you, giving you His *"peace that passeth all understanding."* **(Philippians 4:7)**

#ByFaithWeGood

DAY FOURTEEN

*"The blessing of the Lord, it maketh rich,
and he addeth no sorrow with it."*
Proverbs 10:22 (KJV)

Morning Prayer/Declaration:

"Father, we thank you for a new day to praise your Name. Thank you for your new mercies you have given us today, and every day. God we thank you for welcoming our requests. I thank you Lord that you hear me when I cry out to you. Every day you bless me to see, and I know I can rejoice and be glad in it because I know you have my back. I'm grateful to you for standing up for me and defending me. I can relax, knowing that you're fighting every battle on my behalf and that I can press forward confidently, knowing that you will answer my prayers, according to your will. In Jesus' Name. Amen!"

God's blessings are always for your good, to be enjoyed and shared with others. When God is the head of your life and plans, joy comes with the territory. The blessings of the Lord make you wealthy and prosperous. They make you whole, restore you, are plentiful, and never run out! God's blessings are meant for us to live life more abundantly. The blessing empowers us to succeed, prosper, and be distinguished. When the blessing kicks in, it is no longer your strength…it becomes divine enablement. *Deuteronomy 8:18* says, *"It is GOD who giveth thee power to make wealth,"* meaning that when the blessing is at work in you, your source becomes God. You aren't moved by the state of the economy or your country, neither are you moved by what society and religion think of you. God's blessings empower you to be a blessing in the lives of your family, those around you, and those you are assigned to by God, as well as to live above all of your enemies.

God's covering and blessings make you untouchable and place you in the realm of no limitations. NOTHING is powerful enough to stop you when you're blessed. The blessing of God is His ability conferred on human flesh for unstoppable triumph. All you have to do is to be conscious of it, and walk in it by faith. All that God has done and His blessings are the only gifts that don't come with negative consequences. When the Lord blesses you, there's no sorrow added to it. When He blesses you, He blesses you *all the way*, with no strings attached.

#ByFaithWeGood

DAY FIFTEEN

*"If any of you lack wisdom, let him ask of God,
that giveth to all men liberally, and upbraideth not;
and it shall be given him. But let him ask in faith,
nothing wavering. For he that wavereth is like a wave of the sea
driven with the wind and tossed. For let not that man think
that he shall receive any thing of the Lord.
A double minded man is unstable in all his ways."*
James 1:5-8 (KJV)

Morning Prayer/Declaration:

"Father, thank you for another beautiful, blessed day you allowed me to see. Today and every day, I align my will with your will, which leads to greater understanding and a greater sense of gratitude. God, I thank you for always being available to us, and I declare today that I am available to you. I declare for you to make, shape, mold, prepare, and equip me for where you're leading me and for how you want to use me. In Jesus' Name. Amen!"

Know that we can always ask God for direction when we don't know what to do. We can ask Him in faith, without a shadow of doubt, and He will give us wisdom.

God will not look for a reason not to give you wisdom depending on what you do with it. The Lord wants to give generously! What God has already revealed in the Bible about things like lying and adultery should line up with His answers to prayer; but for the things that are not in the Bible, we should seek the Lord, and ask for wisdom.

Every day of your life, in every situation, in all circumstances, no matter what comes your way, ask God for wisdom. When you ask our Heavenly Father for wisdom, He promises to give it to you without finding fault. God's wisdom will kick in, in every situation, even when you think you aren't prepared to get through a particular issue. As children of God, we use God's wisdom for Kingdom purposes and to do His will. Come what may, God will always come through—for you!

#ByFaithWeGood

DAY **SIXTEEN**

"But the God of all grace, who hath called us unto his eternal glory by Christ Jesus, after that ye have suffered a while, make you perfect, stablish, strengthen, settle you. To him be glory and dominion for ever and ever. Amen."
1 Peter 5:10-11 (KJV)

Morning Prayer/Declaration:

"Father, thank you for who you are. Thank you for another beautiful, blessed day that you have allowed me to see. Lord, teach me what is good. Teach me to be open to you. Teach me to be faithful and committed. Help me to understand your love, your compassion, and your will, so that I may grow and produce the same qualities that you do. You're holy, and you're righteous. Teach me how to be like you. God, I thank you that you are the God of restoration! Knowing no matter what comes my way, I can count on you to restore, strengthen, and make me whole! In your precious and mighty name I pray, Amen!"

Difficulties, hard times, and tough seasons are not always easy to deal with. We never want to go through the process of pressing through tough times, but we are assured that God is with us every step of the way, prepping and equipping us for what is to come…for what He has promised in His Word.

God is the God of restoration, and the only true living God who is able to touch, heal, deliver, and restore. Have strong faith, and know that your season of restoration is coming! He *can* and He *will*!

#ByFaithWeGood

DAY SEVENTEEN

*"The angel of the Lord encampeth round about them
that fear him, and delivereth them.
O taste and see that the Lord is good:
blessed is the man that trusteth in him.
O fear the Lord, ye his saints:
for there is no want to them that fear him."*
Psalms 34:7-9 (KJV)

Morning Prayer/Declaration:

"Father, I come to you humbly to thank you for who you are in my life. For being everything that I need you to be. For being my protector. Thank you for keeping me covered at all times, and for your angels that you have circled around me throughout my day-to-day endeavors. Thank you for being my provider and making sure that I lack no good thing. I continually trust you with my whole heart and I am grateful that you are the head of my life. In the name of your precious Son Jesus I pray. Amen."

Our protection with God is guaranteed because He has us covered in every area of our life. Because of who God is, and the love that He has for us, no hurt, harm, or danger will ever come near us when we press forward in faith. *"O taste and see that the Lord is good."* When you try God for yourself, you'll find out that He's good, He loves you, and you'll be blessed for trusting in Him!

When you show reverence, obey, and respect God for who He is, *"No good thing will He withhold from you."* **(Psalm 84:11 KJV)** It is God's will that we are safe at all times, having all that we need to press forward and never lack. With God, we can *"have life, and life more abundantly." (John 10:10 KJV)*

#ByFaithWeGood

DAY EIGHTEEN

*"But, beloved, be not ignorant of this one thing,
that one day is with the Lord as a thousand years,
and a thousand years as one day. The Lord is not slack
concerning his promise, as some men count slackness;
but is longsuffering to us-ward, not willing that
any should perish, but that all should come to repentance."*
2 Peter 3:8-9 (KJV)

Morning Prayer/Declaration:

"Lord, I thank you for this beautiful day that you've blessed me to see. Another day to experience your goodness in the land of the living. I pray and ask you to forgive me for any and everything I've said, done, or thought about that was not pleasing or pleasant in your sight. I'm grateful to be forgiven and made whole because of your love for me! I declare that as I continue to grow in you, Jesus, my life will reflect you more and more and that today and every day you'll continue to lead, guide, direct, and protect me and my family. In Jesus' mighty Name. Amen."

God is never late, but He is always on time. At times you may feel that what you prayed for and what God has promised is delayed, but God's timing is the best timing. It's our responsibility to stay humble and remain in faith. God loves to give us opportunities to grow closer to Him, to repent of our wrongdoings, and to be ready for His return.

"Seek ye first the Kingdom of God" **(Matthew 6:33 KJV)**, and get into position! Let the Lord lead you, and expect great things.

#ByFaithWeGood

DAY NINETEEN

"Hearing of thy love and faith, which thou hast toward the Lord Jesus, and toward all saints; That the communication of thy faith may become effectual by the acknowledging of every good thing which is in you in Christ Jesus."
Philemon 1:5-6 (KJV)

Morning Prayer/Declaration:

"I decree and declare, God, that I'll have strong faith to serve you and to be faithful and committed to what you've called and created me to do. I thank you for all that I have in you, and that there's no limit with you. I will accomplish all that I set out to accomplish, and I will experience your goodness and be great today, giving you all the honor, glory, and praise. In Jesus' Name. Amen."

When we make the decision to press forward by faith, we become effective for God and those around us, having strong faith to serve and to be committed to the *"yes"* we've given God, producing good fruit with the knowledge of all we have in Christ Jesus.

Have strong faith to be committed to the assignment, purpose, and vision God has given you, and have strong faith to fulfill God's plan on earth. Have strong faith to be an example and reflection of Christ, giving God all the honor, glory, and praise, because with Christ, we have an inheritance that's *guaranteed*.

#ByFaithWeGood

DAY TWENTY

"As ye know how we exhorted and comforted and charged every one of you, as a father doth his children, that ye would walk worthy of God, who hath called you unto his kingdom and glory. For this cause also thank we God without ceasing, because, when ye received the word of God which ye heard of us, ye received it not as the word of men, but as it is in truth, the word of God, which effectually worketh also in you that believe."
1 Thessalonians 2:11-13 (KJV)

Morning Prayer/Declaration:

"Father God, I thank you for who you are in my life. I thank you for this day, knowing that my victory in you is guaranteed. Thank you for the examples you've set through Christ and through your Word. I thank you for how you equip, groom, convict, instruct, and lead me through your Word. I thank You that your Word gives life, and that your Word is at work in me because I believe! In your mighty and precious Son Jesus' Name, I pray. Amen."

The Word of God has been given to us as a guide and a directive as to how we should live. *Nothing* that man says can add to it. God says that His Word is at work in those of us who believe, and when we are in faith, all that God has promised is actively working *in* us and *for* us. God's Word gives *life*. It *heals*. It *delivers*. God's Word *restores*. It *protects*. There is *provision* in the Word. God's Word *equips, grooms, convicts,* and is the *firm foundation* that can *never* be shaken!

"A discerner of the thoughts and intents of the heart." **(Hebrews 4:12)** God's Word *"shall not return unto Him void, but it shall accomplish that which He pleases, and it shall prosper in the thing whereto He sent it."* **(Isaiah 55:11)** And God's Word is at work in those who believe!

#ByFaithWeGood

DAY TWENTY-ONE

*"If ye then be risen with Christ,
seek those things which are above,
where Christ sitteth on the right hand of God.
Set your affection on things above, not on things on the earth.
For ye are dead, and your life is hid with Christ in God."*
Colossians 3:1-3 (KJV)

Morning Prayer/Declaration:

"God I humbly come to you once again, thanking you for another beautiful, blessed day to be great for you, to get in position to prepare for what's coming, and to fulfill your plan in the earth. I decree and declare your Word, "For I reckon that the sufferings of this present time are not worthy to be compared with the glory which shall be revealed in us." **(Romans 8:18 KJV)** *In Jesus' Name, I pray. Amen."*

Everything that we need is in the will of God. There is *nothing* in this world that can satisfy you like God can. We have new life with Christ, and it's *never too late* to start becoming the person God created you to be. For a healthy life, focus and build your life and future on who Jesus is. He says to let our roots grow down in Him because He is what we are meant to be founded on. No one person, place, or thing can fulfill you…only God can. Paul says not only is it important to have a Christ-centered life, but he also shows us how to continue in the calling that you and I have over our lives.

"Take every thought and imagination against the knowledge of God, and bring them into captivity to the obedience of Jesus Christ." (2 Corinthians 10:5 KJV) Don't think like the world…think like Christ. This can only be done by faith…and God is faithful!

#ByFaithWeGood

DAY TWENTY-TWO

"And I will give unto thee the keys of the kingdom of heaven: and whatsoever thou shalt bind on earth shall be bound in heaven: and whatsoever thou shalt loose on earth shall be loosed in heaven."
Matthew 16:19 (KJV)

Morning Prayer/Declaration:

"Lord, thank you for this beautiful, blessed day and thank you for the power and authority that you have given me to control the environment around me. I thank you for the power I obtain from you, that I shall have what I say! From this day forth, I speak life and life more abundantly. I bind everything that is not like you, in Jesus' mighty Name. Amen."

With God, we have the power to control and change our environment. Never allow the enemy and anything that is not from or like God to take root in your life, in your family, around you, and wherever you go. God has given us the power to bind what needs to be bound, and to loose all that God has promised, in Jesus' Name.

Start binding stress, depression, frustration, anxiety, negativity, lack and poverty, sickness, the enemy (who is already defeated!), every demon, witch, and warlock, in Jesus' mighty Name! Declare that *"The joy of the Lord is your strength" (Nehemiah 8:10)*, *"God's peace that passeth all understanding" (Philippians 4:7)*, and every promise that God made be loosed and fulfilled in your life. In Jesus' mighty Name!

#ByFaithWeGood

DAY **TWENTY-THREE**

"Ye are the light of the world. A city that is set on a hill cannot be hid. Neither do men light a candle, and put it under a bushel, but on a candlestick; and it giveth light unto all that are in the house. Let your light so shine before men, that they may see your good works, and glorify your Father which is in heaven."
Matthew 5:14-16 (KJV)

Morning Prayer/Declaration:

"Thank you, Lord, for this beautiful, blessed day you have allowed and blessed me to see! Because of who you are, I thank you that I can press forward by faith this day and every day in confidence, knowing you are with me. I declare that I can be who you, God, created me to be, and I can do what you created me to do. I can go where you created and instructed me to go and be great and fearless, letting your light in me shine before others that they see the good works and give you all the honor, glory, and praise, in Jesus' Name. Amen!"

As believers, we are to be disciples of Jesus Christ and show forth Christ in all of our gifts and talents that God has given us. What Jesus has installed and downloaded in us, we are to use to produce good fruit in a world full of darkness. As believers, we have come to project and provide light to a dying world. When a light shines on a hill, it is for all to see, and we are to live as unhindered light at all times. God will put us in situations where even in the darkest place, we have the light of Christ to shine and reflect Him.

Let your light shine, so that as you lift up the Name of Jesus through your good works, others will be drawn to Him. God's mercy shields us from our trouble and our enemies' hateful work against us. God loves us so much that He has already perfectly planned out every situation and victory in our life. He has started an amazing work in our life that because of His grace, will without a doubt, see through until completion.

#ByFaithWeGood

DAY TWENTY-FOUR

*"And the Lord answered me, and said,
Write the vision, and make it plain upon tables,
that he may run that readeth it. For the vision is yet for an
appointed time, but at the end it shall speak, and not lie:
though it tarry, wait for it; because it will surely come,
it will not tarry."*
Habakkuk 2:2-3 (KJV)

Morning Prayer/Declaration:

"Lord, I come to you grateful, thanking you for another beautiful, blessed day to experience your goodness. I thank you for the plan you have for my life, and that nothing and no one can interfere or get in the way of what you promised. Thank you for preparing the way for me and for making all "the crooked places straight." **(Isaiah 45:2)** *I declare that the plan, purpose, and vision that you have assigned to me will come to pass, and there's nothing the enemy can do about it! In Jesus' Name. Amen!"*

Are you waiting for the desires of your heart to begin to manifest? Are you praying for bondages to break and fall off of you, so that you can see your dreams come to pass? Are you waiting and praying for the salvation of friends and family?

Are you trusting God for prosperity, favor, promotion, honor, and all the blessings found in His Word? Are you tired of waiting for harvest time in your life? Are you frustrated and crying out, *"When, God, when?"* Then you need to understand that God's timing may seem as a mystery, but God's timing is the best timing. He doesn't do things on our timetable. Yet He, through His Word, promises that He will not be late, *not one single day*. God causes things to happen at exactly the right time! Make up your mind that you won't give up until you cross the finish line and are living in the radical, outrageous blessings of God. The more you trust Jesus and keep your eyes focused on Him, the more life you'll have. Trusting God brings life, and believing God brings peace and rest. He delivers on His visions and promises in His own time, no matter how impatient we may get. The vision is what keeps you going when you want to give up and when things are not going as you planned. When you feel like throwing in the towel, you have to remember the vision. In order for you to retain everything God has done and made available to you, you must have a strong passion and remain focused on the purpose and vision God has assigned to you that will change the course of your life for the better.

Writing things down…

- Can help you regain focus on Gods' plan for you.

- Is key to the manifestation. God is still on His original plan.

- Helps you to focus and maintain determination and motivation.

- Becomes the gateway for you. When you write, it forces you to face things. Written plans make things possible.

- Sets things into place. Writing puts the wheels on it, and sets what God promised in motion.

Keep writing, and don't put limits on God.

#ByFaithWeGood

DAY **TWENTY-FIVE**

"Yes indeed, it won't be long now." GOD's Decree.
"Things are going to happen so fast your head will swim, one thing fast on the heels of the other.
You won't be able to keep up. Everything will be happening at once – and everywhere you look, blessings!
Blessings like wine pouring off the mountains and hills. I'll make everything right again for my people Israel: "They'll rebuild their ruined cities. They'll plant vineyards and drink good wine.
They'll work their gardens and eat fresh vegetables.
And I'll plant them, plant them on their own land.
They'll never again be uprooted from the land I've given them."
GOD, your God, says so."
Amos 9:13-15 (MSG)

Morning Prayer/Declaration:

"Lord, I thank you for this day! "This is the day which the Lord hath made; we will rejoice and be glad in it." **(Psalms 118:24 KJV)** *Thank you for your many blessings that have and will overflow in my life! I decree and declare that it is my time and my season for increase, and debt, lack, poverty, setbacks, and delays are no more! In Jesus' Name! "In my prosperity, I shall not be moved."* **(Psalm 30:6)** *Because with you Lord, I'm covered! In Jesus' Name. I pray. Amen."*

As you press forward, know that God will always do exactly what He said He would. Every promise He has made is guaranteed. Because God has promised blessings, they will surely come. Remain focused, faithful, and strong in faith because what you have been praying for, what you have been preparing for…all that you have done up until this point is getting ready to happen.

Your season of promise, restoration, peace, love, joy, happiness, and prosperity is getting ready to happen, so get ready! You are created to win, and God has you covered. There is *nothing* the enemy or anyone else can do about it.

#ByFaithWeGood

DAY TWENTY-SIX

"Surely goodness and mercy shall follow me all the days of my life: and I will dwell in the house of the Lord forever."
Psalm 23:6 (KJV)

Morning Prayer/Declaration:

"God, thank you for how you have me covered. I thank you that I'm never alone, because you are always with me. I thank you for your goodness, your grace, your mercy, and your love that is sufficient, always available, and never-ending. I declare today and every day that I will dwell in your house, in your Word, and with you in prayer all the days of my life, in Jesus' Name. Amen!"

Declare over yourself that God's goodness, mercy, and love shall follow you all the days of your life, in Jesus' Name. Every day, no matter what comes your way, command your day to be great, because God is with you and every*thing* and every *situation* will work for your good.

Let your faith be bigger and stronger than your fears. We are children of the most high God! Children of the King with no limitations! We can move forward without being stopped or blocked, because our victory in Jesus is guaranteed…and there's no limit when God is in it!

#ByFaithWeGood

DAY TWENTY-SEVEN

"And it shall come to pass, if thou shalt hearken diligently unto the voice of the Lord thy God, to observe and to do all his commandments which I command thee this day, that the Lord thy God will set thee on high above all nations of the earth: And all these blessings shall come on thee, and overtake thee, if thou shalt hearken unto the voice of the Lord thy God."
Deuteronomy 28:1-2 (KJV)

Morning Prayer/Declaration:

"Lord, thank you for who you are! It's another beautiful day that you have blessed me to see and I'm grateful to be a part of it. I declare today and every day that I'll follow your lead, be faithful to serve, and obey your voice, because I believe, as it says in your Word, that "obedience brings blessings, and disobedience brings curses." **(Deuteronomy 11:26-28 KJV)** *Have your way in my life, in Jesus' mighty Name. Amen!"*

Obedience is *"the practical acceptance of the authority and will of God."* It includes submitting to Him and then expressing that submission in actions, words, and thoughts. To be obedient is to be in agreement with God, and to be in agreement with God is to be in a position of power in Christ. Disobedience is caused by rebellion and distrust of God. To be disobedient is to yield to self-will instead of surrendering to God and desiring His will in all things. God expects obedience. *(Deuteronomy 11:26-28)* To choose Christ is to choose obedience. *(John 14:15, 21)* To become disobedient is to sin or rebel against God. *(I Samuel 15:22-23)*

Declare to God today by faith, *"For thou art my rock and my fortress; therefore for thy name's sake lead me, and guide me." (Psalm 31:3 KJV)* Pressing from the old and stepping into the new, let the Lord lead you and expect the blessings and promises of the Lord to manifest in your life.

#ByFaithWeGood

DAY TWENTY-EIGHT

"Now unto him that is able to keep you from falling, and to present you faultless before the presence of his glory with exceeding joy, To the only wise God our Savior, be glory and majesty, dominion and power, both now and ever. Amen." **Jude 1:24-25 (KJV)**

Morning Prayer/Declaration:

"Father, I thank you for each day you bless me to see and be a part of. I'm grateful that you are a keeper, and that I'm kept by you! Thank you that I can press forward today and every day, confidently knowing that with you, God, I'm kept to persevere, win, and be victorious! Kept to have all I need, to be great for you, giving you all the honor, glory, and praise in Jesus' Mighty Name. Amen!"

Keep: *"To have or retain possession of. Continue, or cause to continue in a specified condition, position, or course."*

Kept: *"To retain one's place in or against opposition or difficulty." "Guarded and protected."*

Persevere: *"Continue a course of action even in the face of difficulty."*

Family, God is a *preserver*! He will keep you if you want to be kept. In this chapter of *Jude*, the apostle exhorts us to remain steadfast in faith. Christians, we are called to be *in* the world, but not to be *of* the world. We are called out of the world from the evil spirit and temper of it (Satan). We're called above the world to higher, bigger, and better things, to heaven, things unseen and eternal, called from sin to Christ, called from uncleanness to holiness, to live a life where mercy, peace, and love are ours in abundance. This according to the divine purpose and grace of and through our Lord Jesus Christ. God protects, He guards, He preserves, and He watches. God is the keeper who is ALWAYS there. He doesn't take a break or go on vacation. Not only is God always on the job, but He is also aware of when we are having a difficult time in our lives. We can look back at past difficulties and see how God was our keeper all along, protecting and preserving us through all of life's difficulties. The Lord told me to say to those of you who…

- Are struggling and thinking that this year would be no different…

- Think that you cannot go on with your Christian walk because sometimes it is so hard to do the right thing…

- Are bound by the circumstances of your life…

- Are trapped in a relationship that has you living outside of the will of God…

- Have made a resolution to serve God from now on, but the devil has already told you that things will not change for you, that you will go on like before, and that you may even try to start doing right; but it would not be long before you fall flat on your face, going back to your old ways…

Family, the Lord told me to tell you that Jesus is able to keep you from falling!

"Let my soul be at rest again, for the Lord has been good to me." **(Psalm 116:7 NLT)** We can rest in The Lord because He's faithful, and He never abandons us. We can rest in The Lord because He's been better to us than we've been to ourselves, and because *"The Lord is good, and His mercy endureth forever."* **(Psalm 136:1 KJV)**

#ByFaithWeGood

DAY **TWENTY-NINE**

"That if thou shalt confess with thy mouth the Lord Jesus, and shalt believe in thine heart that God hath raised him from the dead, thou shalt be saved. For with the heart man believeth unto righteousness; and with the mouth confession is made unto salvation."
Romans 10:9-10 (KJV)

Morning Prayer/Declaration:

"Father, today as I press forward, I thank you for what you've done through your Son Jesus Christ, and I declare today, that I want to get to know you more. Forgive me for all my sins and for falling short of your glory. Forgive me for everything I've said, done, and thought about that was not pleasant or pleasing in your sight. I declare today that I accept your Son Jesus Christ as my Lord and Savior. Jesus, save me and come into my heart. Come into my life, and have your way. I declare that today is the first day of the best days of the rest of my life, in Jesus' Name. Amen!"

If you have been reading this devotional and now want to receive and experience who God is for yourself and position yourself to *"cast all your care on Him, because He cares for you."* **(Peter 5:7 KJV)** I encourage you to accept Jesus Christ into your life as your Lord and Savior! Falling in love with Jesus was the best thing that ever happened to me, and when you accept Christ into your life, you'll also be a witness that falling in love with Jesus is the best thing that ever happened to you, and this day will be the beginning of the best days of the rest of your life!

God freely adopts us into His eternal family. Open up your heart today, and invite Jesus into your life and into all of your circumstances. Accept, believe, and confess that Jesus is your Lord and Savior and you shall be saved.

#ByFaithWeGood

DAY **THIRTY**

"For there is no difference between the Jew and the Greek: for the same Lord over all is rich unto all that call upon him. For whosoever shall call upon the name of the Lord shall be saved."
Romans 10:12-13 (KJV)

Morning Prayer/Declaration:

"Lord, thank you so much for this beautiful, blessed day. Thank you, that no matter where I am or the time of the day that I can call on your great name by faith, early in the morning, in the noon day, or late in the midnight hour, and you'll always show up for me! To save, to set free, to heal, to deliver, to restore, to protect, and to make whole all who call on your great name. I love you with my whole heart, and I'm grateful that you are the head of my life. In your great name Jesus, I pray, Amen!"

The name of Jesus is used on a daily basis. But do we actually take time out to think about what His Name *means*? Throughout the Bible, we see 'in Jesus' Name' or 'in My Name' and it leads us to wonder...*what exactly is so special about this name?* It is the Name of Jesus that is able to save us! As it says in **(Romans 10:13)** *"Whosoever calls on the name of the Lord will be saved."*

The Name that is able to heal us! *(Acts 3:16)* The Name that even demons are afraid of! *(Luke 10:17)* The Name that is above every name! *(Philippians 2:9 KJV)* The Name that every knee shall bow, every tongue shall confess that Jesus is Lord! *(Philippians 2:10-11 KJV)* Whoever believes in Jesus will not be disappointed! The ultimate goal, what we should seek the most, is to have a personal relationship with Jesus Christ! There's absolutely nobody like Him! There's nobody greater than our God!

The foundation of our faith isn't just *what* we believe; it's *who* we believe *in*. God's people are reunited with Him through one name. The broken and hurting are healed by one name. The lost are found in one name. And that name is *Jesus*! We draw all our strength from Him. We discover our calling in Him. We define our purpose through Him. Jesus is the center of it all. When calling upon the Name of Jesus becomes our natural response to anything life brings us, we build our lives upon a foundation that can never be shaken. And no matter what the enemy tries, you ought to use the power God has installed in your voice; and declare that in the Name of Jesus and through His blood and power, the devil is hereby evicted from my life!

#ByFaithWeGood

DAY **THIRTY-ONE**

"Brethren, I count not myself to have apprehended:
but this one thing I do, forgetting those things which are behind,
and reaching forth unto those things which are before,
I press toward the mark for the prize of
the high calling of God in Christ Jesus."
Philippians 3:13-14 (KJV)

Morning Prayer/Declaration:

"Lord, thank you that I can press forward in this day and every day knowing you already have my victory set up, and that all I have to do is just press toward it by faith, going confidently in the direction that you're leading me. I declare today that no matter what comes my way, I'll keep pressing, keep praising, keep praying, because with you, God, we always win! In Jesus' mighty Name. Amen!"

God doesn't want us to look to the past, but to move on, stay focused, and let nothing and no one interfere. It takes courage and it can be hard sometimes; but keep *pressing*, keep *praising*, and keep *praying*. By faith, continually press towards the promises of God, and know that your victory is guaranteed!

Walking by faith is never giving up on your dreams; the vision and purpose that God has assigned to you to fulfill. It is believing without a doubt that God has a greater plan for your life. So *"be ye steadfast, unmovable, always abounding in the work of the Lord."* (**1 Corinthians 15:58 KJV**) Believe without a doubt that God has a greater plan for your life, then get ready, get in position, and let the Lord lead you as you expect great things.

#ByFaithWeGood

How to Press Forward, By Faith

Throughout life, because of tough times and circumstances, pressing forward may seem difficult. With the influences in this world, staying focused is necessary in order to press forward in the way that God is leading you. Pressing forward by faith takes focus, commitment, dedication, and hard work. It takes having a strong passion for the will of God, for where He's leading you, and for how He wants to use you to fulfill the purpose He assigned to you and receive all that He has promised you. To experience who God is, to accomplish the goals you set, as well as using the gifts He has given you takes strong passion and the determination to press forward by faith.

To press forward by faith means having a mindset focused on knowing God has already given you the victory, and you just have to press toward it, going confidently in the direction that He is leading you! God is a present help, and He's not focused on your past. Sometimes, you may self-sabotage living the desires of your heart, and become distracted in the way God created you to press forward, simply because of what happened in your past. But remember family, God created you for His good purpose, already knowing the beginning from the end, and He is still your present help in a time of need. God doesn't want us to look to the past, but to move on, staying focused, and not allowing ourselves to be influenced to get off course.

*Pressing forward by faith means to
press forward by any means necessary!*

Pressing forward by faith is not always easy; but with God, it's always worth it. It takes putting in the work, getting and being equipped, and learning what you need to learn, getting inspired, so that you're not frustrated because of how situations look or what is going on around you. Pressing forward by faith is a *mindset*. Pressing forward by faith is living according to the Word of God and having a bond and relationship with Him that *can* never…*will* never…be broken. It is loving God with your whole heart, because you know Him for yourself. When pressing forward by faith, your focus is to always put God first, believing in who He is without any doubt or worry…because by faith, you'll always have *what* you need, as *much* as you need, every *time* there's a need! *(2 Corinthians 9:8 NIV)* By faith, your victory in Jesus is always guaranteed!

How to Press Forward Through All Challenges

Challenges. We don't always like them. Some are more complex than others, and you may have moments of frustration, anxiety, or feeling as though you're alone and have to try and figure things out by yourself. At times, even though we know what our responsibility is, we choose not to pray, read, and meditate on God's Word because reality kicks in and we get fed up. It is easy to feel as though you've been waiting too long, dealing with the same challenges, struggles, and tough circumstances...and nothing is changing.

Family, the Lord told me to remind you in this devotional that God's grace is *more than enough* to meet every challenge that we face. **(2 Corinthians 12:9 NIV)** His resources are unlimited and by the grace of God, *"we can do anything, through Christ who strengthens us!"* **(Philippians 4:13 paraphrase mine)** God created us to be victorious in every area of our lives. We are created to be overcomers and achievers, functioning by faith as more than conquerors through Jesus Christ **(Romans 8:37)**, who loves us continually and unconditionally.

Although we have challenges, they are never meant to hinder or set us back. Challenges are never times for us to give up, but opportunities for us to learn and become stronger as we press forward. **Hebrews 10:23 (KJV)** says, *"Let us hold fast the profession of our faith without wavering; (for he is faithful that promised;)"* When challenges come, it's our responsibility to *get* in position, *stay* in position, and *own* our position, taking ownership of who God has created us to be and for what He has called and created us to do. God is faithful, and He is a promise keeper. God is *always* with you, even when it doesn't feel like it! He said He will *"never leave you, nor forsake you."*

(Hebrews 13:5 KJV) *"God is not a man, so he does not lie. He is not human, so he does not change his mind. Has he ever spoken and failed to act? Has he ever promised and not carried it through?"* **(Numbers 23:19 NLT)** To press forward by faith through challenges, you have stay focused and stand firm on the Word of God and His promises.

2 Corinthians 5:7: "For we walk by faith, not by sight." How we press through challenges is based on our focus. Come what may, no matter what it looks like, press forward by faith, believing that it's already done. By faith, your situation is already handled, and what you need is already in place. God has already worked it out for your good according to His will. Believe by faith that God is always with you and has you covered in all areas of your life, and there's nothing that the enemy can do about it.

---

*Don't let what you **see** dictate what you **believe**!*

When challenges, struggles, and tough circumstances arise, we are not to press forward according to what we *see* (how the situation looks), but press forward by faith because of *what we know God said in His Word*. Which is why we all have to have the Word of God established in us. We are created to live according to God's Word, not what we see, or *"leaning to our own understanding." **(Proverbs 3:5-6 KJV)*** Pressing forward by faith through our challenges means we must be determined, never give up, and never give in, but believing through faith that God is always able. We must have strong faith to be healed…to be delivered…for provision…for doors to open…to overcome, knowing that because God is the greatest power, we will never be defeated! ***(Jeremiah 10:12 and 1 Chronicles 29:11)***

"Who is he that overcometh the world, but he that believeth that Jesus is the Son of God?" **1 John 5:4 -5 KJV**

We are created to overcome through Christ Jesus who gave us the victory, knowing that with and through Christ, we can overcome every situation. Every problem. Every obstacle. Every trial and tribulation…and especially every challenge. We overcome because of who we are in Christ, not because of what we do or have. We overcome because we are born of God, and we are born of God because we believe that Jesus Christ is the Son of God.

As you read earlier, pressing forward and walking by faith is a mindset. We must have a "made-up mind" that says no longer will we compromise or conform to situations just because they arise and take place in our life. God has given us power, authority, and everything that we need (our gifts and abilities) to take control and rise above every challenge. Pressing through all challenges is to seek God above all else, as well as seeking to be where He is, pressing through all challenges to be a finisher and remaining determined to finish what you started, accomplishing every goal you set, to fulfill the purpose God assigned to you, positioning yourself for God to finish what He started in you. Why? Because *"Being confident of this very thing, that he which hath begun a good work in you will perform it until the day of Jesus Christ."* **(Philippians 1:6 KJV)** God is always working on your behalf, and He always will, until the day Jesus Christ returns. God can and will sustain you in ways beyond what you can imagine. Pressing through all challenges is standing firm on God's Word by faith. Family, know that you're going to finish stronger than where you started. God's love never gives up, never runs out, and it is always available!

How to Press Forward to Be Exactly Who God Created You to Be

When it comes to you and me, God reveals through His Word the nature and identity of becoming a Born-again believer in Christ Jesus; those who have their lives devoted to God's call and His purposes.

"But ye are a chosen generation, a royal priesthood, a holy nation, a peculiar people; that ye should shew forth the praises of him who hath called you out of darkness into his marvelous light."
1 Peter 2:9 (KJV)

"For thou hast possessed my reins: thou hast covered me in my mother's womb. I will praise thee; for I am fearfully and wonderfully made: marvelous are thy works; and that my soul knoweth right well."
Psalm 139:13-14 KJV

Many times throughout God's Word, He describes who He created us to be. We are created with a purpose. To be *strong and courageous* **(Joshua 1:9)**, and walk confidently in who we are. Because of the influences in this world, we may find ourselves trying to fit in or be popular, which becomes a battle and at times can become a distraction.

God made you in the way He wants you to be and exactly who He wants you to be, and He loves you too much to allow you to stay tied to any*one* or any*thing* that does not bring out the best in you.

Because of who God is, you can declare over yourself: *I am who God said I am, and I can be who God said and created me to be. I can do what God said I can do and I can have all that God said I can have,* according to His will, because there is no limit with God, and there is nothing that the enemy or anyone else can do about it, in Jesus' Name!

Family, you are fearfully and wonderfully made, and everything you need to be great in the sight of God…to be successful as a child of God and become the person that He wants you to be…is within you. You are *equipped, blessed, talented,* and *empowered,* and because of that, you can be *focused, bold,* and *confident,* not holding back but giving God praise for who He is and for all of the great things He's done.

"And be not conformed to this world: but be ye transformed by the renewing of your mind, that ye may prove what is that good, and acceptable, and perfect, will of God." **Romans 12:2 KJV**

One way of renewing your mind is to shut off the comments that others have made about you and replace them with what God says about you in His Word. Pressing forward to be exactly who God created you to be is knowing who you are. Not getting caught in the opinions of others, not compromising or downplaying who you are, but being unapologetically great for God, standing out in humility. When you allow God to transform and change you, you'll realize how awesome you really are, because you are a child of

God. You will see how blessed you are, how prosperous you are and can be, how special you are, and once again, that you can be confident. You understand how talented and healthy you are, and how you can be spiritual and happy.

Jesus lives inside of each one of us, and He always has our best interest at heart. We were created in the image of God, and we don't have to settle for less or accept being treated badly because of who we are. Some people may take our humility and the fact that we are a nice person as a sign of weakness.

Recognize your worth. You are a child of the Most High God, who is predestined for greatness! Whose focus and faith is in the Lord and not what others may think about you. Start expecting great things! You are created to enjoy being who God created you to be. You are special and unique, created to live and declare the works of the Lord. *(Psalm 118:17 KJV)* Get in position! Stay in position! Own your position!

How to Press Forward to Win!

Winning. Everyone wants to win. The great thing about all of us and winning is that everybody *can* win. We're created to win. Created to *"live life and life more abundantly"* **(John 10:10 KJV)**, enjoying the plan and purpose of God. God wants you to be confident in the truth that, through Him, *"All things are possible."* **(Matthew 19:26 KJV)** You can be confident in the truth that God is pouring His strength into you. And young people, as you get older, you will understand as well. Pray that God gives you the strength to overcome whatever challenges you may face! God has plans for each and every one of us, but at times, we may become contrary and buck against them. We may grumble and complain, but we must realize that God knows best. He is in control of our lives (and we should always desire Him to be so), especially since He knows what tomorrow holds. He sees the future and therefore knows what is best for us. *Our* purpose is to fulfill *God's* purpose.

"Wherefore take unto you the whole armour of God, that ye may be able to withstand in the evil day, and having done all, to stand. Stand therefore, having your loins girt about with truth, and having on the breastplate of righteousness; And your feet shod with the preparation of the gospel of peace; Above all, taking the shield of faith, wherewith ye shall be able to quench all the fiery darts of the wicked." **Ephesians 6:13-16 (KJV)**

As believers, we are called to make an impact with our lives; however, in order to do that effectively, we must *stand firm*, so that we can *stand out* for God. We need God's mighty power to help us remain strong in our faith, as well as to make God's power effective in our lives. We must remember that the devil is out to *"kill, steal, and destroy." (John 10:10)* The devil is always plotting, and he will trip us up when we least expect it. This is why we need to put on *all* of God's armor. The *belt* of truth. The *breastplate* of righteousness. Our *feet shod* with the preparation of the gospel of peace. The *shield* of faith. The *helmet* of salvation. The *sword* of the Spirit. And *always being in prayer, so that we can withstand the spiritual attacks from the devil*, because God's will and purpose is that we live a life of VICTORY and maximize our life to its fullest potential.

"But thanks be to God, which giveth us the victory through our Lord Jesus Christ."
1 Corinthians 15:57 (KJV)

---

*Faith is...not knowing **what the future holds**, but knowing **who holds the future**. Faith is...not just believing that God **can**, but also knowing that God **will**!*

> *"Now thanks be unto God, which always causeth us to triumph in Christ, and maketh manifest the savor of his knowledge by us in every place."*
> **2 Corinthians 2:14 (KJV)**

It's amazing what you can overcome when you believe what God has promised. He is not holding anything back, and He has promised that He will set us free. He assures us total overcoming victory in our life because He is a promise keeper. You can expect the favor of God to be in full manifestation in your life. It doesn't really matter who you *used* to be...all that matters is *who you are becoming* because of where God is leading you in your life.

God is preparing you for new blessings as you press forward! That means you've got to let go of some things, people, and habits. It may be difficult; but when God starts to move in your life, you will realize that it was all worth it!

> *"There is therefore now no condemnation to them which are in Christ Jesus, who walk not after the flesh, but after the Spirit."*
> **Romans 8:1 (KJV)**

Salvation is available to all of us. There is nothing you can do to escape God's grace when you accept the Lord Jesus Christ as your personal Savior.

"You were not created to live a depressed, defeated, guilty, condemned, ashamed, or unworthy life. You were created to be VICTORIOUS!" ~Joel Osteen

No matter where you are or what you may go through... remember to LIVE WELL! LAUGH OFTEN! LOVE MUCH! Be encouraged, and press forward! Your circumstances cannot change God and who He is. If God is *all you have*, then you have *all you need*. We are victorious, no matter what the situation looks like. With God, we've already won! You are loved and created to win. You have been equipped, qualified, anointed, and appointed to let your light shine for God! We've got Jesus, and we should be glad about it! Come what may, God makes us win!

My Testimony

God is so good in allowing me to share my journey and all that He has done and is doing, to give Him all the glory and to encourage you all. In 2017, led by God, I stepped out in faith. People judged and criticized me for doing it, but it was my obedience to God that mattered. I began to work with a great team of people on some major projects, including working with an investor, developing business plans, working on the vision God blessed us with to include music, ministry, education, and so much more. Everything was focused on advancing God's Kingdom. I began to focus on putting in the work and fulfilling the purpose that God assigned to me, even though I struggled financially and was living back at my mom's house.

I continued to stay focused and be faithful in what God assigned me to do, going through the process (which seemed like it was taking forever). My faith was strong, and I did not get out of position. I had moments where I felt discouraged, wondering when, where, and how it was all going to come together and dealing with the personal opinions of others — but I knew that God would get me through it all. I had to shake off my feelings and continue to press forward, keeping myself encouraged and my faith in God and His Word strong.

When God confirmed my decision, I moved from Philadelphia to Chicago. The team that I was working with wasn't happy about my decision; and although I wanted to work things out, we could not come to an agreement, and they decided to move forward without me. After all the hard work that I had put in over the last three years, I found myself starting all over again. Even though I had put in a lot of time with that team and on those projects, with God's Word, and the support and encouragement of my wife and family, I started fresh with creating and developing. I look back from where I was to where I am; from struggling, putting in the work, and believing God for the results, to living in a whole different state and being married to my beautiful wife, Vanessa. We have a beautiful luxury one-bedroom apartment, and we are looking forward to becoming homeowners soon! I got a new car, so my wife and I now have our own vehicles. Doors are opening. I have been blessed to publish this devotional, and I'm still putting in the work. I've accomplished a lot but still have a lot more to do, and I am looking forward to what's ahead. God is so AMAZING!

I'm sharing my testimony to encourage you to Never. Give. Up. Keep going, and God will always come through for you. Stay focused, and keep your faith in God and His Word strong. Where God leads you in life is *always* greater than where you've been! To God be all the glory!

Conclusion

There may have been some rough times for you as well; but through it all, God has been with you every step of the way, and in spite of everything, it's all worth it.

I'm forever grateful for how God used me to lift Him up and to encourage and pray for you all throughout this devotional, all for His Glory! I pray that every word has truly been a blessing to you. As you press forward, I will continue to encourage and pray for you as God allows me to. It is not about us, but it is and always will be all about Jesus! *His* will. *His* way. *His* plan. *His* purpose. *His* desire. Seeking what God wants more than what we want. In conclusion, I am so looking forward to what God has in store for all of us in the years to come. All of the hard work and preparation is going to pay off, and it only gets better from here. And come what may, it's *always* going to work for our good.

For the last three years, the Lord has blessed me to livestream and lead His children in prayer every Thursday night at 7:00 p.m. (EST) on Facebook, Instagram, and YouTube, to encourage and be a blessing through prayer. I'm praying that every prayer posted will encourage you all to press forward by faith, knowing that God is always with you, and He'll always have you covered. I pray that you will give God all of the glory!

Testimonials

"I thank God for Minister Marrow and his obedience to what God has blessed him to do. I enjoy reading the morning messages from him. I don't always read them right away...sometimes, I sit and read them all together and go over the Scriptures. They encourage me and help me to strengthen my faith and deal with situations that come my way. God is so good!

By the grace of God and His goodness, He has instilled in His people like Minister Marrow the ability to comfort us with His Word. I look for Scriptures that you send to us every weekday morning to keep encouraging us and keep us on the straight and narrow challenges of life." **~Antonia Batts, Philadelphia, PA**

"I'm grateful to God for Minister Marrow sending out the morning texts and inspiration. They really help me to stay focused and get through my days at work. The people at my job could be a lot to deal with at times, but God uses Minister Marrow every morning to encourage me and give me strength to stay focused and keep going." **~First Lady Tonia Moore, New Salem Baptist Church, Philadelphia, PA**

"Wow! I needed this encouragement today because I'm in a health program that I know I really need, but I was thinking about giving up. With tears in my eyes, Minister Marrow, I thank you for being faithful to God and His Word! Have a marvelous day!" **~Dr. Latonya Smalls, Jubilee Worship Center, Friendship, MD**

"I thank God for Minister Marrow sending out the word every morning. They help start my day and are so confirming! It's such a joy to receive them!" ~**Deacon Earl Ransom, Temple of Divine Love Church, Philadelphia, PA**

"You are truly an amazing man of God. I pray every morning and thank God for waking me up, for my health, and for the health of my children. While watching you live, I have prayed that God would bless me with a man like you; someone who loves God and is not ashamed to praise Him. I am in a difficult relationship right now, and I cannot wait for it to be over. I want to start going to church and change my life. I want my kids to grow up in church. I am glad that I can reach out to you. I really appreciate you and what you do for the Lord because it is changing me.

You are amazing, and I am so happy to have met you. I believe that it was God who put you in my life and sent you as a messenger to help me. I thank Him for you every day!" ~**Mariana Sanchez, Philadelphia, PA**

About the Ministry

I received the message to begin **ByFaithWeGood Ministry** in early 2016. One day I was sharing the daily post (words of encouragement and inspiration) which I always ended with a few hashtags. The Lord gave me the hashtag *#ByFaithWeGood* and it stuck with me.

I began to use *#ByFaithWeGood* in all of my daily posts of encouragement and inspiration. Because I was faithful with it, God gave me a vision for **BFWG Ministry**. By using it constantly, God began to download the vision in me for the hashtag *#ByFaithWeGood* and it officially became a ministry.

The ministry includes:

- Preaching and teaching
- Workshops, seminars, and concerts
- Online sermon series and panel discussions
- Daily posts of morning encouragement and inspiration
- Monday Motivational Moments
- Thursday night prayer LIVE and the prayer line
- *The ByFaithWeGood* podcast

#ByFaithWeGood is not just a hashtag…it is a movement. A ministry to encourage all of God's children to:

- Be strong in their faith and to stay grounded in God's Word
- Believe in His Word and who He is without wavering
- Receive and experience all of His promises
- Take ownership of who He has created each of us to be

By doing these things, we can be sure that God receives all of the honor, glory, and praise, lifting up the name of Jesus, so that all others around us will be drawn closer to Him by our example.

As I pressed forward in building the **ByFaithWeGood** ministry (a nonprofit organization), I began to build on another vision the Lord revealed to me, by extending the **ByFaithWeGood** ministry into **ByFaithWeGood Productions LLC**. Both are focused on bringing together music and ministry, including:

- music and creative production
- collaborations and outreach ministry
- providing resources and funding sowing into the purpose of others
- hosting community/charity events and networking expos
- and much more...

The ultimate goal is to assist God's children in using their creative gifts to produce good fruit that will encourage and inspire themselves and others, drawing all of His children closer to Him and giving God all of the glory.

We look forward to keeping you informed as the ministry expands in advancing God's Kingdom!

By Faith We Good - BFWGMinistry Mission Statement

"Bringing all of God's children together, equipping them to be strong in faith, always being grounded in God's Word, advancing God's Kingdom. Walking by faith and not by sight."
(2 Corinthians 5:7 KJV)

Minister Bernard Marrow
Founder/President
BFWG Ministry

ByFaithWeGood
"For we walk by faith! Not by sight!"

About the Author

Morning Devotionals "Inspired to Press Forward"
31 Devotions & Declarations That Will Inspire You to Press Forward, By Faith

Many people preach about faith…and even more proclaim that they are living by faith…but a life of faith requires that you press forward despite the challenges.

In his debut book, Minister Bernard Marrow has provided a resource for believers to use every day to help them stay focused and grounded in God and His Word.

Inside the pages of this book you will discover relevant Scriptures, inspirational readings, and daily empowerment…so that you can walk by faith!

Minister Bernard Marrow is an admirable, faithful steward of God, whose unique style and daily devotions will connect readers with the heart of God...he has provided a literary gem for today's world to "press forward."
>   ~**Deacon Jermaine Worthy, New Salem Baptist Church, Philadelphia, PA**

After reading this book, I am even more inspired to continue to press forward by faith, and I believe this book will motivate you to do the same.
>   ~**Evangelist Cheryl A. Johnson, Founder and President, The Women in the Word Ministries Philadelphia, PA**

I thank God for Minister Marrow and his obedience to what God has blessed him to do. I enjoy reading the morning messages from him...they encourage me and help me to strengthen my faith and deal with situations that come my way.
>   ~*Antonia Batts, Philadelphia, PA*

...The people at my job can be a lot to deal with at times, but God uses Minister Marrow every morning to encourage me and give me strength to stay focused and keep going.
>   ~**First Lady Tonia Moore, New Salem Baptist Church, Philadelphia, PA**

I thank God for Minister Marrow sending out the word every morning. They help start my day and are so confirming! It's such a joy to receive them!
>   ~**Deacon Earl Ransom, Temple of Divine Love Church, Philadelphia, PA**

Minister Bernard Marrow, a native of Philadelphia, Pennsylvania, is the founder and president of ByFaithWeGood – BFWG Ministry. He is a singer, songwriter, musician, minister, and a faithful hard worker, who accepted the Lord as his Savior at an early age and became a member of New Salem Baptist Church, where he was adopted by Pastor Robert Moore as his spiritual son and mentee. Minister Bernard received his ministerial license in April of 2014 and currently resides in Chicago, Illinois with his beautiful wife, Vanessa.

"I can do all things through Christ which strengthens me."
Philippians 4:13 KJV

"I believe that this Scripture should be our daily confession. God wants us to be confident in the truth that through Him, all things are possible."
~Minister B. Marrow

Connect with the Author

Facebook:
https://www.facebook.com/bernard.marrow.1

ByFaithWeGood on Facebook:
https://www.facebook.com/BFWGMinistry/

Instagram:
https://www.instagram.com/min.marrow/

ByFaithWeGood Instagram:
@bfwgministry

Snapchat:
Min. Marrow

Twitter:
@MinMarrow
ByFaithWeGood: @ByFaithWeGood

Email:
connectwithmin.marrow@gmail.com

ByFaithWeGood:
BFWGMinistry@protonmail.com

Website:
www.BFWGMinistry.com

www.ingramcontent.com/pod-product-compliance
Lightning Source LLC
Chambersburg PA
CBHW051406290426
44108CB00015B/2177